ALWAYS LOVED

DEVOTIONAL SERIES

EXPERIENCING THE FATHER'S TENDERNESS
THROUGH EVERY SEASON OF LIFE

AUTUMN
A Time to Reflect

BRENT LOKKER

ALWAYS LOVED DEVOTIONAL SERIES
AUTUMN

ISBN: 978-0-9882164-4-0

Cover design & interior layout | Yvonne Parks | www.PearCreative.ca

Autumn

A TIME TO REFLECT

With the arrival of autumn we eagerly embrace the early rains as a much-needed respite from the heat of summer. These are the times when the soil of our hearts is quenched with a much-needed drink of the goodness of our Father. The autumn holidays tend to draw families together, even for a short period of time where laughter rings out. We're reminded again of what's most important in our lives—taking time to express our love for each other. Autumn is a time of reflection, when we place before our Father areas of our lives that may need tending to. Oh, and autumn also brings winds of change. But remember that roots grow deep when the winds are strong.

People of Zion, shout with joy and happiness in the Eternal, your God; The drought is over; He has sent the early autumn rain as a sign of His faithfulness. He has poured down heavy rain, autumn and spring, as before.

JOEL 2:23 (VOICE)

May he be like rain falling on a mown field, like showers watering the earth.

PSALM 72:6 (NIV)

God blesses the soil which drinks in the rain that often falls on it and which grows plants that are useful to those for whom it is cultivated.

HEBREWS 6:7 (GNT)

You'll notice I use several different names for God in this devotional. I call Him Father, Papa, and even Daddy. I encourage you to know God, not as a distant, angry or indifferent Father, but as a close, kind and warm Father who loves to be with you. If being so tender and informal with Him is new for you or even makes you uncomfortable, I encourage you to read my book *Always Loved: You are God's Treasure, Not His Project.*

Each week in this devotional you'll start by reading tender words from your heavenly Father, along with an encouragement from the Bible. I want you to re-read those same tender words every day of the week, allowing them to go deeper and deeper into your heart. Reading them out loud is especially helpful. I'll also ask you to respond to a question each day or have you engage with Papa's heart in one way or another. There's a half page of lines upon which to write your thoughts in response, but I've also left the bottom half of the page blank in case you would rather draw a picture or doodle in a way that speaks to the creativity within you.

The final day of each week I ask you to *do something that's life-giving and to do it together with your heavenly Father*. Why do I ask you to do this? We're often so serious we forget to have fun along the way. Doing things you enjoy that bring more life to your heart is a significant part of God's plan for your life. So give yourself permission to do something life-giving (i.e. do a puzzle, make cookies, call an old friend, listen to music that inspires you, go on a hike and enjoy nature, etc.) but invite your Father to do it with you. When you're aware of Him enjoying life with you, whatever you're doing is enhanced.

Having said all that, since life is an adventure with Papa and not a test, I encourage you to use this devotional in whatever way helps you feel close to Him. After all, that is the goal!

Enjoy the journey into the depths of Papa's huge heart for you as His treasured child!

WEEK 1

I've Always Loved You

My son, My daughter, I'm your Father and you belong to Me. I wanted you and chose you for Myself before you were born. You have always been Mine and you will always be Mine. I will never change My mind. No one can take you away from Me. Ever! I love you, My child! Hear My heart. I've always loved you! Let Me draw you in closer. Please don't pull back from My complete acceptance of you. My love is the greatest force in the cosmos and it's fully fixed upon you as My heart's true desire!

I want you to feel secure in every way with Me— for you to know that nothing will ever come between our love for each other. I'll speak words of tenderness and affirmation to affirm My heart for you. My kindness and acceptance will completely transform your life. I am the safe, adoring Daddy you've needed your whole life, and I'm here to shower you with My affection. Come in closer and hear My voice of approval.

READING FOR WEEK ONE

You can tell for sure that you are now fully adopted as his own children because God sent the Spirit of his Son into our lives crying out, "Papa! Father!" Doesn't that privilege of intimate conversation with God make it plain that you are not a slave, but a child? And if you are a child, you're also an heir, with complete access to the inheritance.

GALATIANS 4:6-7 (MSG)

I have loved you with an everlasting love and so I still maintain my faithful love for you.

JEREMIAH 31:3 (NJB)

Each day this week, re-read Papa's kind words to you again, then go deeper by writing down or drawing your responses to the following questions:

DAY 1

What's the first response of your heart to these words from your Father?

DAY 2

How does it feel to be wanted, chosen and loved before you could do anything? Talk with Papa about it, being honest about the places in your heart that may still feel like this is too good to be true. What do you want to do with those feelings that don't line up with the truth of what your Father says is true?

DAY 3

The deeper you've been hurt in life, the more you might try to sabotage relationships as a way to protect your heart out of fear that those relationships won't last. Let your Father's complete acceptance of you wash away the fears of rejection and pain. He wants to hold you and comfort you. Will you let Him do that?

DAY 4

You are God's true heart's desire. Desire means He wants to be with you and longs to be close to you. Do you believe Papa desires you? Let Him go to any places within you that don't feel desirable or loveable.

DAY 5

God is your safe Daddy who longs for you to feel totally secure in His love. Did you feel secure with your earthly parents? How has that helped or hurt your ability to experience the security of God's love for you? Open your heart up—cry if you need to. Talk with Him about the security you've always needed.

DAY 6

Your Father wants you to hear His voice of approval. Did you hear approval growing up? Papa can and will make up for anything you may have lacked growing up. Listen to His quiet voice within and write down His words of approval. Be sure to hear His approval for you as His child and not just for the good things you do. What do you hear Him saying?

DAY 7

Do something that's life-giving today and do it together with your heavenly Father. Journal it or draw it here at the end of the day.

WEEK 2

I Like You

My child, you may think I love you because I have to, but I love you because you're loveable. I made you that way. And you know what else? I like you! Yes, you! I like everything I made about you—the color of your eyes, your infectious laugh, even what you think is your quirky personality—everything! I like hanging out with you, whether we're doing something or doing nothing together. I enjoy looking at you because you make Me smile. Simply being with you brings Me tremendous happiness and joy.

You need to know I'm not irritated with you or putting up with you. You're not My project, you're My treasure. I want you to like yourself, too. There are so many reasons why. If those reasons are hard for you to come up with, just ask Me. I'll tell you. It's time that we enjoy life a whole lot more together.

READING FOR WEEK TWO

He does not merely tolerate you politely,
He delights Himself in you!

EPHESIANS 5:29 (TMT)

Each day this week, re-read Papa's kind words to you again, then go deeper by writing down or drawing your responses to the following questions:

DAY 1

What's the first response of your heart to these words from your Father?

DAY 2

Growing up, did anyone give you the false message you were a bother to them? A constant irritation? Papa wants you to know something very different. He values you and He's very interested in your thoughts, ideas and dreams. Why don't you share them with Him right now.

DAY 3

Can you think of ways you just being you makes your heavenly Papa smile? Write them down or draw them.

DAY 4

Do you have some memories of spending time with a good friend? Write down one of them if you remember. God is your Father but also the best of friends who thoroughly enjoys you. Can you remember some fun times you've had with Him? Write one of those times down. If this is new for you, ask Him to help you create fun memories together.

DAY 5

Ask your heavenly Dad to help you come up with a whole page full of reasons to like yourself. He'd love to help you!

DAY 6

What would need to change for you to enjoy life a whole lot more with your heavenly Father? A change in perspective? Removing fear? Whatever it is, write it down or draw it here and then ask Papa to bring about that change. Let Him know you want to enjoy life the way you were meant to.

DAY 7

Do something that's life-giving today and do it together with your heavenly Father. Journal it or draw it here at the end of the day.

WEEK 3

See the Bigger Picture

Step back a moment, My child, and see the bigger picture from My perfect perspective. Before a single day of your life came to pass, I knew each and every moment that would take place. I'm at the beginning and I'm at the end, and I'm at every point in between at the same time. Every moment in time is now for Me. Therefore, I'm already with you at the finish line of your life as well as in eternity, and I like what I see!

I've given you a free will to make decisions that will cause certain outcomes. Yet, I've already taken those decisions and outcomes into account. As only I can do, I weave even poor choices into something beautiful as you open up to Me and let My light in. I'm bigger than your mistakes! I have no "plan B" for your life, only My singular "plan A" to do phenomenally good things for you just as I promised I would. There are many more chapters ahead of you that you haven't yet lived. I can't tell you all about them yet, but I will sometimes give you future glimpses so you'll know they're filled with hope and promise.

You'll have to trust in My ability and desire to successfully maneuver you through life's circumstances in such a way that the end result is breathtaking. Child, climb up onto My lap and see the whole picture as I see it with the sealed-up victory of your life in plain view!

READING FOR WEEK THREE

You saw me before I was born and scheduled each day of my life before I began to breathe. Every day was recorded in your book!

PSALM 139:16 (TLB)

So we are convinced that every detail of our lives is continually woven together to fit into God's perfect plan of bringing good into our lives, for we are his lovers who have been called to fulfill his designed purpose.

ROMANS 8:28 (TPT)

God is the one who began this good work in you, and I am certain that he won't stop before it is complete on the day that Christ Jesus returns.

PHILIPPIANS 1: 6 (CEV)

Each day this week, re-read Papa's kind words to you again, then go deeper by writing down or drawing your responses to the following questions:

DAY 1

What's the first response of your heart to these words from your Father?

DAY 2

Have you been anxious lately about your life and how it's all going to work out? Tell your Father all about it and ask Him for His perspective. Write down or draw what you sense from Him.

DAY 3

Papa says, "I'm bigger than your mistakes." Imagine your life lived in that truth. Living in the regret of past mistakes keeps you trapped in a bad place. It's time to forgive yourself and move into the best days of your life that are ahead of you. Do that now if you need to and talk with God about your future of hope and promise that's your inheritance.

DAY 4

God works all things together for your good. All things means *all things*! Are there troubling things happening in your life right now where this promise seems impossible for God to keep? Make a choice to lay down your ability to make sense of it all and place these things into His able hands. Craft this into a prayer below and pray this as often as you need to along the way.

DAY 5

Ask your Father if there are any glimpses of what is to come in the chapters ahead in your life He wants to show you. He will do that sometimes, but always to give you hope. Write down or draw the impressions that come to you.

DAY 6

Choose to believe God that when you look back at your life with Him, it will be beautifully breathtaking. Speaking of which, take a deep breath and trust in Papa's ability and desire to lead you through your life. Close your eyes and see yourself on His lap as He beams at you and laughs with joy over the brilliance that is your life. Write down or draw what you experience.

DAY 7

Do something that's life-giving today and do it together with your heavenly Father. Journal it or draw it here at the end of the day.

WEEK 4
Whose Report Will You Believe?

I've chosen you as My blessed and highly favored child and I've made you a light in the midst of darkness. I'm highlighting you to the world. I'm on the throne at all times and in every situation, both in your life and throughout the earth.

The world says to you, "Fret! Be anxious!"
But I say to you, "Peace. Be still."

The world says to you, "Lose sleep worrying! All is lost!" But I say to you, "I'm with you and I'm for you. I'm orchestrating a much greater good than what you can see. All is going according to My brilliant plan."

Oh, My child, I give you My peace that surpasses your own understanding. That means you'll have to give up your demand to have everything all figured out in your mind. That's still you trying to take care of you, which is exhausting. My Spirit and your spirit are connected all the time. Instead of being led by your own reasoning and perception, listen to My Spirit within you who restores your emotions and your thinking back into their proper alignment of peace. Take a deep breath. All is well!

READING FOR WEEK FOUR

The ways of right-living people glow with light; the longer they live, the brighter they shine.

PROVERBS 4:18 (MSG)

Don't be pulled in different directions or worried about a thing. Be saturated in prayer throughout each day, offering your faith-filled requests before God with overflowing gratitude. Tell him every detail of your life, then God's wonderful peace that transcends human understanding, will make the answers known to you through Jesus Christ.

PHILIPPIANS 4:6–7 (NIV)

Peace I leave with you. My peace I give to you. I do not give to you as the world gives. Do not let your hearts be troubled and do not be afraid!"

JOHN 14:27 (NIV)

Each day this week, re-read Papa's kind words to you again, then go deeper by writing down or drawing your responses to the following questions:

DAY 1

What's the first response of your heart to these words from your Father?

DAY 2

In what current situations in your life or in the world do you need to have God's assurance He's on the throne? Talk with Him about it and write down your impressions of His response to you.

DAY 3

Since expressing overflowing gratitude is such a big part of not worrying, take some time right now to make a list of (or draw) what you are thankful for. Then go over the list, truly letting the gratitude spill out of your heart to your Father.

DAY 4

Where are you feeling fatigued and overwhelmed still trying to take care of yourself? Agree with Papa's ability to do so. Pour out your heart to Him here and let Him calm you down with His tenderness towards you.

DAY 5

Has your mind been working overtime to figure out solutions to problems that seem to overwhelm you? Your mind was designed brilliantly to access information stored there, but it's God's Spirit who has all the answers you need. He feeds the answers to your spirit, which can then relay them to your brain.

DAY 6

Say out loud, "It is well with my soul. I will not be troubled or afraid. I have God's peace deep within me." Keep going with these positive, truthful declarations and write them down. Agreeing with God's truth changes your perceptions.

DAY 7

Do something that's life-giving today and do it together with your heavenly Father. Journal it or draw it here at the end of the day.

WEEK 5

Spirit-to-Spirit Communication

My Spirit is communing with yours continuously. There's never a time when we're not connected in this significant way. If you aren't perceiving My gentle communication with you just yet, keep asking for Me to help you understand My spirit language and go easy on yourself since it takes time to learn.

Though I'm communicating with you in many ways, it's rarely in an audible way. This is a Spirit-to-spirit encounter, which means it's something you sense from deep within. Instead of dismissing this as your own thoughts, you will begin to understand I'm feeding you sweet truths from My heart to yours. I will reveal Myself to you in ways that are unique to you and Me—sometimes even with inside jokes just for you and Me!

READING FOR WEEK FIVE

The Spirit, not content to flit around on the surface, dives into the depths of God, and brings out what God planned all along. Who ever knows what you're thinking and planning except you yourself? The same with God—except that he not only knows what he's thinking, but he lets us in on it. God offers a full report on the gifts of life and salvation that he is giving us. We don't have to rely on the world's guesses and opinions. We didn't learn this by reading books or going to school; we learned it from God, who taught us person-to-person through Jesus, and we're passing it on to you in the same firsthand, personal way. Spirit can be known only by spirit—God's Spirit and our spirits in open communion. Spiritually alive, we have access to everything God's Spirit is doing, and can't be judged by unspiritual critics. Isaiah's question, "Is there anyone around who knows God's Spirit, anyone who knows what he is doing?" has been answered: Christ knows, and we have Christ's Spirit.

1 CORINTHIANS 2:10-15 MSG)

Morning by morning, he makes my ear alert to listen like a disciple. Lord Yahweh has opened my ear and I have not resisted, I have not turned away.

(ISAIAH 50:4-5 NJB)

Each day this week, re-read Papa's kind words to you again, then go deeper by writing down or drawing your responses to the following questions:

DAY 1

What's the first response of your heart to these words from your Father?

DAY 2

You are connected all the time with your heavenly Father in a significant way. Since we are so often longing for deeper connection with others, talk with Papa about what this connection means to you.

DAY 3

Do you find yourself frustrated that you don't hear God, or that you don't hear Him as clearly as you want to? His "language" with you is mostly internal—Spirit to spirit, a knowing of things you did not know a moment before. Ask for His help to pick up more clearly the multitude of ways He's communicating with you. Write that prayer here.

DAY 4

Faith is intriguing. You first believe *then* you see, not the other way around. Write or draw your declarations that you DO hear from God and you DO know His assuring voice (even if you are *feeling* otherwise). This act of faith is a doorway into greater realms of communication with your Father. Please trust me on this one and make the declarations.

DAY 5

Pray this prayer: "Holy Spirit, tell me what's on the heart of my Father right now. I will be still and listen." Then, in faith, write down (or draw) what you sense from within and don't dismiss it as your own thoughts. For those who are concerned you won't hear God correctly, please trust that God's Spirit can help you discern what is and is not His voice—what's more important right now is that you believe you do hear from Him.

DAY 6

God can speak with you through Bible verses, through songs on the radio, or even through a billboard or other advertisement you see while driving. Look for those opportunities today to hear Him communicate with you and remember to write down or draw what you sensed from Him. As your heart is more and more in tune with Him, you will discover just how sweetly your Father is continuously communing with you.

DAY 7

Do something that's life-giving today and do it together with your heavenly Father. Journal it or draw it here at the end of the day.

WEEK 6

Revealing Hidden Truths

I long to share more and more of the hidden truths of My kingdom with the ones who want deep relationship with Me. That includes you, My precious child! These are powerful secrets from the depths of My being that I only reveal to those who share My heart and desires. There are no bad or shameful secrets in My kingdom, just hidden truths reserved for those who want to go deeper with Me. Get to know Me even more. I'm kinder than you can imagine and even better than what you have known Me to be. But find out for yourself why that's true. Choose to want to know the depth of My heart, even if it feels a bit scary at first to do so. The hidden truths I reveal about My kingdom will never lead you into fear, but always into greater realms of My peace, assurance and justice.

I have such plans for you, My child—plans to enrich the world through you … plans to bring My freedom to others … plans to draw you in deeper and to have you sit longer in My refreshing, restoring presence. Allow Me to share the depth of My heart with you. What do you want to know about My heart?

READING FOR WEEK SIX

It is the greatness of God to keep things hidden, but it is the greatness of kings to find things out.

PROVERBS 25:2 (NLV)

'For I know the plans I have for you,' declares the Lord, 'plans to prosper you and not to harm you, plans to give you hope and a future.'

JEREMIAH 29:11 (NIV)

Each day this week, re-read Papa's kind words to you again, then go deeper by writing down or drawing your responses to the following questions:

DAY 1

What's the first response of your heart to these words from your Father?

DAY 2

Your heavenly Father doesn't have any bad secrets to keep from you, only deeper truths He loves to reveal to those who want to know Him. If you had shameful secrets you were forced to keep earlier in life, talk with Papa about them and let Him remove any shame or anxiety associated with them. Write down your interaction.

DAY 3

What's it like for you to have a Papa who trusts you to share the deeper things on His heart with you? Tell Him how that impacts and heals your heart.

DAY 4

What deeper truths does your heart want to know about your heavenly Father? Ask Him! He's longing to share with you.

DAY 5

Do you believe you are royalty and that it's part of your inheritance to search out the treasures of God? What adventure as a king or queen are you prepared to take with Him? Let your heart wander and then write or draw your thoughts here:

DAY 6

Justice—making wrong things right—is a huge theme in God's kingdom. If there are wrongs in this world where you long to see God's justice, ask Him to reveal hidden truths and answers that you can begin to pray or to live out to bring heaven's justice. Write down your interaction as well as any steps the Lord is encouraging you to take.

DAY 7

Do something that's life-giving today and do it together with your heavenly Father. Journal it or draw it here at the end of the day.

WEEK 7

I Supply Everything You Need

I supply everything you need and then some because it brings Me great joy to do so. Faith is never about striving harder or approaching Me in just the right manner to get what you need. Faith is choosing to trust in the goodness of My heart, just like a little child who knows his daddy will take care of him. In My grace covenant with you established by Jesus' death on the cross, everything that belonged to Jesus is now yours—including His faith! The key to enjoying all that's yours as My loved and favored child is to keep looking at Jesus' sufficiency, not at what you perceive your deficiencies to be. Constantly focusing on how you think you're doing is a recipe for disaster. Instead, ask Me what I see. I may show you areas in your life that aren't consistent with your complete new nature in Christ, but I will always do so in a way that encourages you and fills you with hope. And when I do show you an area that requires an upgrade by applying the truth of the cross, I want you to ask Me to do it because I'm the only One who can.

READING FOR WEEK SEVEN

The conclusion is clear: the original rest is still left in place for God's people. God's rest celebrates His finished work. Whoever enters into God's rest immediately quits his own efforts to add to or complement what God has already perfected.

HEBREWS 4:9–10 (TMT)

You satisfy my every desire with good things. You've supercharged my life so that I soar again like a flying eagle in the sky!

PSALM 103:5 (TPT)

Each day this week, re-read Papa's kind words to you again, then go deeper by writing down or drawing your responses to the following questions:

DAY 1

What's the first response of your heart to these words from your Father?

DAY 2

A small child does not wonder where her next meal is coming from. The food simply "appears" on the table. Though her mother or father works hard to make that possible, all she knows is that her immediate needs are met. Your heavenly Papa is inviting you to live this way again. Transcribe the cry of your heart to live in this childlike manner deeply trusting your Daddy to care for you.

DAY 3

What are your true needs? Lay these before your Papa and let your heart be convinced of His deep desire and ability to take care of those needs.

DAY 4

Papa God says to you, "My child, you have much greater faith than you imagine. No matter what's happened in your life, you know there's no one else to turn to but Me. That's faith!"

DAY 5

Invite Papa to show you areas in your life that aren't consistent with who you truly are as a new creation in Christ. Allow Him to give you an upgrade! Complete this prayer in any way He leads you: "Father, do for me what I can't do for myself and take me into the good places You've designed for me to go…"

DAY 6

Ask for God's help to enter into the rest of what He's completed for you that will allow you to soar high in the sky like an eagle. Imagine yourself as that eagle, flying above the concerns down below. What's it like in His carefree presence?

DAY 7

Do something that's life-giving today and do it together with your heavenly Father. Journal it or draw it here at the end of the day.

WEEK 8
Risk Loving Again

I understand the deep pain you've lived through because of damaging relationships in your life. I know how you'd rather pull back from people because of the disappointments you've experienced in your past. But without the risks of loving you also won't experience the rewards of loving. The pinnacle of life is to love and be loved.

I'm also aware of how your own immaturities have added to the pain of relationships, even if you've been unaware. I want to heal your heart and help you grow so you can enjoy healthy relationships the way you long to. If you feel you've made a mess of your life and your relationships, you need to know I specialize in turning things around and restoring what you may think is beyond repair. I am so much bigger than your mistakes!

And in the midst of it all, you need to know I am for you as well as for the ones who have caused you pain. I will never choose one of My children over another. Instead, I will choose to pursue every single one of My children with the same passion. That's what love does. Please choose to bless and not curse those who've hurt you. Ask Me to bless their lives and heal their hearts. It's what I specialize in doing.

Look for a fresh season of healthier, more life-giving relationships. Risk loving again and enjoy the immense rewards of being loved.

READING FOR WEEK EIGHT

Love is patient with people. Love is kind.
There is no envy in love; there are no proud claims;
there is no conceit.
Love never does the graceless thing; never insists on its rights,
never irritably loses its temper;
never nurses its wrath to keep it warm.
Love finds nothing to be glad about when someone goes wrong,
but it is glad when truth is glad.
Love can stand any kind of treatment; love's first instinct is
to believe in people;
love never regards anyone or anything as hopeless; nothing can
happen that can break love's spirit.
Love lasts forever.

1 CORINTHIANS 13:4-8 (BARCLAY)

Each day this week, re-read Papa's kind words to you again, then go deeper by writing down or drawing your responses to the following questions:

DAY 1

What's the first response of your heart to these words from your Father?

DAY 2

Ask God what are the walls, if any, you've put up in relationships in an attempt to protect yourself from being hurt. Have a good chat with Papa about why they are there and why you feel you need them. Having these honest conversations with Him is so healthy!

DAY 3

Since constructing your own walls for safety is exhausting, ask God if He has something better in mind. Find out what He would give to you in exchange for you letting go of your own methods of protecting your heart. Be sure to journal this exchange

DAY 4

Ask God to show you any areas of immaturity in your own life that have added to the pain of relationships. Understand that He will never shame you, only help you. If Papa shows you an area that needs healing, tell Him you are willing for Him to change you and ask if there's anything He wants you to do. Write these things down.

DAY 5

How does it feel to know God is bigger than your past mistakes? Since He specializes in turning things around and restoring your life, it's time to let go of any past mistakes that may still be causing you to feel shame. Do that right now and receive His mercy and forgiveness.

DAY 6

Is there anyone who's hurt you in the past who you need to bless instead of curse? In addition to forgiving others, choosing to bless them is extremely liberating. It's okay if you don't have warm fuzzies in your heart as you do this. Just know that Papa is listening and so very proud of you!

DAY 7

Do something that's life-giving today and do it together with your heavenly Father. Journal it or draw it here at the end of the day.

WEEK 9

I Will Never Cut You Off

I'm never looking for reasons to cut you off because I can't and I won't. Resist falling into the performance-based trap of religion. If you don't fully understand My covenant of grace with you, you'll wear yourself out trying to be good enough and do enough right things for Me, believing this to be the essence of the Christian life. I am far better than that. Our relationship is built on love and love alone! My perfect love can't and won't cut you off.

It's My choice to bless you and not to curse you. It's My choice to do good to you and display My outrageous favor upon you every day of your life. It's My choice to love you extravagantly because I want to. I've purposed this to be the way it is, and I will always make good on My promise.

It's never My heart to cut you off, but always My heart to graft you in. You are wanted and included in My family, now and always!

READING FOR WEEK NINE

By entering through faith into what God has always wanted to do for us—set us right with him, make us fit for him—we have it all together with God because of our Master Jesus. And that's not all: We throw open our doors to God and discover at the same moment that he has already thrown open his door to us. We find ourselves standing where we always hoped we might stand—out in the wide-open spaces of God's grace and glory, standing tall and shouting our praise.

ROMANS 5:1–2 (MSG)

Each day this week, re-read Papa's kind words to you again, then go deeper by writing down or drawing your responses to the following questions:

DAY 1

What's the first response of your heart to these words from your Father?

DAY 2

Have you ever had thoughts that God is looking for reasons to cut you off? Share your fears with Him and let Him bring comfort to your heart.

DAY 3

Are there any ways in which you've found yourself falling back into the trap of religion—being good enough for God? Pour out your heart to the One who longs to remove that unrealistic pressure from your life.

DAY 4

Grace is God doing for you what you could never do for yourself in a million years. It's the opposite of performance. Papa invites you into the covenant of grace that Jesus purchased for you to live in, where you are accepted as His child long before you could do anything to earn it. Accept His grace right here and right now…

DAY 5

God's choice is exactly that—His and His alone. Talk with Him about the myriad of ways He's chosen to bless your life and the kindness of His heart to want to do so.

DAY 6

One of our deepest needs is to be included. What emotions do you feel as you discover Papa has already thrown open His doors to you because He always wanted you? Let Him know.

DAY 7

Do something that's life-giving today and do it together with your heavenly Father. Journal it or draw it here at the end of the day.

WEEK 10

I've Planted a Dream Inside You

Long, long ago, as your forever Father, I wanted you to exist so I would have you to lavish My love on. And long, long ago, as your forever Father, I planted a dream inside of you that would be fulfilled in the time I determined you would be born and alive to walk on the earth. While I've place dreams within each of My children to enjoy closeness with Me and to release My transforming love and joy, My dream for you is perfectly unique. This dream isn't something you have to figure out—it's already woven into the essence of who I've made you to be. It's the very thing that brings you life and happiness when you're immersed in it. I want you to discover the creativity and distinct voice I've given you to make a difference in this world. You represent My heart unlike anyone else. Now, I want you to release it, unashamedly, with all you've got! Since no one else can replace you, the world is richer because of you. Will you believe Me?

READING FOR WEEK TEN

For we are the product of His hand, heaven's poetry etched on lives, created in the Anointed, Jesus, to accomplish the good works God arranged long ago.

EPHESIANS 2:10 (VOICE)

God can do anything, you know—far more than you could ever imagine or guess or request in your wildest dreams! He does it not by pushing us around but by working within us, his Spirit deeply and gently within us.

EPHESIANS 3:20 (MSG)

Each day this week, re-read Papa's kind words to you again, then go deeper by writing down or drawing your responses to the following questions:

DAY 1

What's the first response of your heart to these words from your Father?

DAY 2

Tell Papa how it feels (or draw a picture) to have His dream already woven inside of you.

DAY 3

What were your hopes and dreams as a little child? Daydream with Papa about those days of yesteryear and then write or draw what you remember.

DAY 4

Figuring out what we're alive to do is simpler than what we make it. What is it that makes you come alive and brings you true joy? Write it down (or draw it) and talk with God about it.

DAY 5

If you had no limitations and could do whatever brought you joy, what would you be doing? Ask God to help you take at least one intentional step today in this direction. Write down what brings you joy and what step you are taking.

DAY 6

Some of you have been fed the lie that your voice isn't important. You were born to be heard and to make a positive difference. Ask Papa for your voice back. Start using it right here to make strong declarations for why you're alive, unashamedly!

DAY 7

Do something that's life-giving today and do it together with your heavenly Father. Journal it or draw it here at the end of the day.

WEEK 11
My Banner Over You is Love

My favored child, I've brought you into My presence to sit and dine with Me at My banqueting table. You are not My servant waiting upon Me at the table. You are My friend and special guest. What's Mine is yours! And while we're enjoying each other's company, look up and beam at My banner of love over you. This banner is a huge flag that I hoist up and wildly wave over you. The love that's embroidered into it leaves splashes of My affection and approval for you as it rips through the air, trumpeting the finality of our choice to belong to one another. Our union and togetherness has been sealed forever because of the victory of Jesus on the cross.

I'm filled with inexpressible joy and laughter, reveling in the unchangeable status of you and I engaged in an eternal gaze of mutual adoration. The power of My words of loving affirmation continually wash over you, making you whole and holy. This causes you to be radiant, beaming with confidence. And My radiant ones will transform the earth by sharing My love and affection with others. So look up and see how My banner of love over you shouts out the unchanging truth of My heart for you..

READING FOR WEEK ELEVEN

He placed me at his banquet table, for everyone to see that his banner over me declares his love.

SONG OF SONGS 2:4 (VOICE)

You are wholly beautiful, My beloved, and without a blemish...you ravish My heart with a single one of your glances.

SONG OF SONGS 4:7, 9 (NJB)

Christ's love makes the church whole. His words evoke her beauty. Everything he does and says is designed to bring the best out of her, dressing her in dazzling white silk, radiant with holiness.

EPHESIANS 5:26-27 (MSG)

Each day this week, re-read Papa's kind words to you again, then go deeper by writing down or drawing your responses to the following questions:

DAY 1

What's the first response of your heart to these words from your Father?

DAY 2

Do you ever feel you are only supposed to approach God as a servant? How does it impact you to know you've been invited to sit and dine with Him instead of serving the food?

DAY 3

Picture yourself at the Lord's banqueting table. Let your God-inspired imagination go there. How exquisite is it? What foods are spread out before you? Most importantly, where is the seat of honor for you? Have fun with this, describing or drawing it.

DAY 4

Once again, use your God-inspired imagination to look up at this banner of love that cascades over you. What does it look like? What images are on it? What colors streak through the air? How does it make you feel? Talk with Papa about it.

DAY 5

Do you need a fresh washing of affirming words over you today? Papa is more than happy to oblige. Ask Him again, "What do You think of me?" and "When You look at me, what do You see!" Get ready for a deluge of affirming truth and write down or draw what you sense from His sweet voice.

DAY 6

As a beaming radiant one, you transform the earth through the power of God's love and affection for each person you meet. Ask Him for one of those encounters today with someone who needs to be shown this love and affection. Write down what happens at the end of the day. Remember, even the smallest act of love and kindness has huge ripple effects in God's kingdom.

DAY 7

Do something that's life-giving today and do it together with your heavenly Father. Journal it or draw it here at the end of the day.

WEEK 12

Rivers of Living Water

There is a river that flows from My heart to yours and never runs dry. It flows from My throne and courses right through you to refresh and rejuvenate you. Feel the tension, anxiety, fear and depression drift away as it's replaced with My righteousness, peace, love and joy. Why don't you stop right now for a moment and enjoy the constant current of My heavenly river that's flowing through you?

Immerse yourself in this river—not just ankle-deep, but go in further where the water level is saturating you. In the times of your life when you've felt disappointment that My blessings seem to be flowing away from you, be sure you are turned upstream towards My face. Sometimes the cares of life have worn you out and caused you to look away from Me downstream. Turn upstream again and see that My blessings are streaming right towards you! I know how to be sure those blessings get to you.

READING FOR WEEK TWELVE

There is a River whose waters make glad the city of God, the holy place where the Most High lives.

PSALM 46:4 (NLV)

My heavenly guide brought me to the river of pure living waters, shimmering as brilliantly as crystal. It flowed out from the throne of God and of the Lamb.

REVELATION 22:1 (VOICE)

Jesus stood and shouted to the crowd: 'All you thirsty ones, come to me! Come to me and drink! Believe in me, so that rivers of living water will burst out from within you; flowing from your innermost being, just like the Scripture says!'

JOHN 7:37-38 (TPT)

Each day this week, re-read Papa's kind words to you again, then go deeper by writing down or drawing your responses to the following questions:

DAY 1

What's the first response of your heart to these words from your Father?

DAY 2

Each day this week, I want you to visit this river, picturing and feeling the current coursing right through you. What needs to be washed away? What is being restored? Be sure to turn upstream and see the delight in your heavenly Father's face towards you. His blessings are streaming right towards you continuously! Each day, ask God to take this experience to a higher level. Record what happens.

DAY 3

Each day this week, I want you to visit this river, picturing and feeling the current coursing right through you. What needs to be washed away? What is being restored? Be sure to turn upstream and see the delight in your heavenly Father's face towards you. His blessings are streaming right towards you continuously! Each day, ask God to take this experience to a higher level. Record what happens

DAY 4

Each day this week, I want you to visit this river, picturing and feeling the current coursing right through you. What needs to be washed away? What is being restored? Be sure to turn upstream and see the delight in your heavenly Father's face towards you. His blessings are streaming right towards you continuously! Each day, ask God to take this experience to a higher level. Record what happens.

DAY 5

Each day this week, I want you to visit this river, picturing and feeling the current coursing right through you. What needs to be washed away? What is being restored? Be sure to turn upstream and see the delight in your heavenly Father's face towards you. His blessings are streaming right towards you continuously! Each day, ask God to take this experience to a higher level. Record what happens.

DAY 6

Each day this week, I want you to visit this river, picturing and feeling the current coursing right through you. What needs to be washed away? What is being restored? Be sure to turn upstream and see the delight in your heavenly Father's face towards you. His blessings are streaming right towards you continuously! Each day, ask God to take this experience to a higher level. Record what happens. Ask for the rivers of living water that you've been experiencing this week to burst forth from within you.

DAY 7

Do something that's life-giving today and do it together with your heavenly Father. Journal it or draw it here at the end of the day.

WEEK 13

My Truth Sets You Free

There are many voices screaming at you, but only One Shepherd's voice that will always lead you to green pastures. I know how to give you the rest your soul needs and how to lead you in the best direction.

Listen to the truth of My voice that replaces and washes away the lies. Knowing truth the way I declare it to you is your true freedom. The more you believe My heart for you the way it really is, the less you will be tormented by thoughts that do not come from Me.

I'm not putting up with you and I'm not put off by you. I'm captivated, enamored, fascinated, and smitten with you. Because I'm fully committed to you, I'm positioning you for success, even using what you would think are failures to launch you into the destiny I've designed for you.

I do not see "character flaws" in you; I see the splendor of My perfect creation when I look at you. I am lovingly removing anything that would dim the light of My glory through you. While some would say there are no superstars, I want to remind you that My Son, Jesus, is the never-ending Supernova exploding from within you, making you an infinitely bright star in a galaxy of like-shining stars. As you display My light and life and freely give it away to others, you bring Me great joy and delight.

And never forget that I love you this very moment and every moment of our forever lives together.

READING FOR WEEK THIRTEEN

God, my shepherd!
I don't need a thing.
You have bedded me down in lush meadows,
you find me quiet pools to drink from.
True to your word,
you let me catch my breath
and send me in the right direction.
Your beauty and love chase after me
every day of my life.
I'm back home in the house of God
for the rest of my life.

PSALM 23:1-3,6 (MSG)

Then you will experience for yourselves the truth, and the truth will set you free.

JOHN 8:3 (MSG)

Each day this week, re-read Papa's kind words to you again, then go deeper by writing down or drawing your responses to the following questions:

DAY 1

What's the first response of your heart to these words from your Father?

DAY 2

Have you been feeling worn out lately? Allow your Good Shepherd to bring you back into lush meadows and to drink from quiet pools. Quiet your heart right now and experience how real this is. Afterwards, write or draw your experience.

DAY 3

Have you been tormented lately with thoughts that cause anxiety or cause your mind to race incessantly? Lay those before Papa and ask for His truth to replace them. Write it down so you can come back to the truth whenever you need to.

DAY 4

Every time you are tempted to beat yourself up over something, reflect on the truth that God doesn't see character flaws in you. He only sees His perfect creation. In what areas do you need to apply this truth to experience freedom? Talk with your Daddy who adores you.

DAY 5

Are you aware of Jesus within you, His brilliance exploding out through you to a world of people longing for His truth? Ask Him for a greater awareness of His glorious presence within you. What's He showing you?

DAY 6

One of the greatest of all truths is to know that God's beauty and love chase after you every day of your life. Every day! There is no time, no circumstance, and no situation that changes this truth. Repeat this slowly multiple times: "Father, Your beauty and love chase after me every day of my life!" As this goes in deeper, record your thoughts.

DAY 7

Do something that's life-giving today and do it together with your heavenly Father. Journal it or draw it here at the end of the day.

I bless you in your ongoing and ever-deepening walk with your heavenly Papa. He so admires your courage to allow Him into the painful places of your heart so He can heal you and breathe fresh life and hope through you. Remember that after autumn's reflection comes winter's nurturing. Your Father is building a history with you, moment by moment, of His enduring faithfulness. He will never leave you nor forsake you. He cannot, for you are His dear, dear child and He will shower His kindness upon you all the days of your life. Now that's a Father you can spend your lifetime enjoying!

With Much Love,

Brent

Made in the USA
Lexington, KY
17 September 2017